MICHIGAN

HELLO
U.S.A.

by Karen Sirvaitis

Lerner Publications Company

You'll find this picture of apple blossoms at the beginning of each chapter in this book. The apple blossom was chosen as Michigan's state flower in 1897 because of the many apple trees that grew there. Apple trees still grow all over Michigan. In 2000 the state's 8.56 million apple trees produced 850 million pounds of apples.

Cover (left): The Mackinac Bridge. Cover (right): Cars on an assembly line in Sterling Heights, Michigan. Pages 2–3: Detroit skyline. Page 3: Tulips in Holland, Michigan.

The publisher wishes to thank Pesky and The Kid for their ongoing inspiration for this title.

This book is available in two editions:
Library binding by Lerner Publications Company, a division of Lerner Publishing Group
Soft cover by First Avenue Editions, an imprint of Lerner Publishing Group
241 First Avenue North
Minneapolis, MN 55401 U.S.A.

Website address: www.lernerbooks.com

Library of Congress Cataloging-in-Publication Data

Sirvaitis, Karen, 1961–
　　Michigan / by Karen Sirvaitis. (Rev. and expanded 2nd ed.)
　　　p.　cm. — (Hello U.S.A.)
　　Includes index.
　　Summary: An introduction to the land, history, people, economy, and environment of Michigan.
　　ISBN: 0–8225–4085–1 (lib. bdg. : alk. paper)
　　ISBN: 0–8225–0783–8 (pbk. : alk. paper)
　　1. Michigan—Juvenile literature. [1. Michigan.] I. Title. II. Series.
F566.3 .S57 2002
977.4—dc21　　　　　　　　　　　　　　　　　　　　　　　　　　　2001006133

Manufactured in the United States of America
1 2 3 4 5 6 – JR – 07 06 05 04 03 02

CONTENTS

Water along the lakeshore freezes during a cold Michigan winter.

THE LAND

The Great Lakes State

ne of Michigan's many nicknames is the Great Lakes State. Superior, Huron, Erie, and Michigan—four of the five **Great Lakes**—border Michigan. Lake Ontario, located about 130 miles east of Michigan, is the only Great Lake that does not touch this midwestern state.

Michigan is divided into two **peninsulas,** or pieces of land surrounded by water on three sides. The Upper Peninsula (often called by its initials, the U.P.) borders Wisconsin and the Canadian province of Ontario. The Lower Peninsula also borders Ontario, as well as the states of Indiana and Ohio. The Straits of Mackinac, a narrow waterway joining Lakes Michigan and Huron, separates the two peninsulas.

Spanning the Straits of Mackinac, the Mackinac Bridge connects the Upper and Lower Peninsulas.

Isle Royale
National Park

N
W   E
S

MICHIGAN
Political Map

⭐ State capital

0   25   50 Miles

0   25   50   75   100 Kilometers

Marquette •

Munising •

Seney •

Sault Sainte
Marie •

Empire •

Traverse City •

Shepherd •

Bad Axe •

Saginaw •
• Frankenmuth

Cedar Springs •

• Flint

Grand Rapids •
Holland •

⭐ **Lansing**

Pontiac •

Highland Park •
• Warren
• Detroit

Kalamazoo •

Battle
Creek •

Jackson •

Dearborn •

Milan •

• Brownstown

The drawing of Michigan on this page is called
a political map. It shows features created by
people, including cities, railways, and parks.
The map on the facing page is called a physical
map. It shows physical features of Michigan,
such as coasts, islands, mountains, rivers, and
lakes. The colors represent a range of elevations,
or heights above sea level (see legend box).
This map also shows the geographical regions
of Michigan.

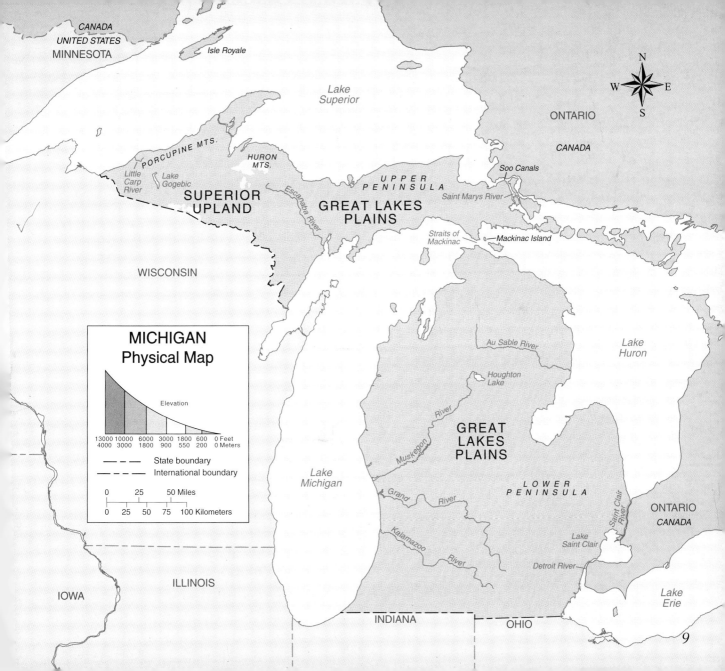

CANADA
UNITED STATES
MINNESOTA

Isle Royale

Lake
Superior

N
W   E
S

ONTARIO

CANADA

PORCUPINE MTS.

HURON
MTS.

Soo Canals

Little
Carp
River

Lake
Gogebic

U P P E R
P E N I N S U L A

SUPERIOR
UPLAND

GREAT LAKES
PLAINS

Escanaba River

Saint Marys River

Straits of
Mackinac

Mackinac Island

WISCONSIN

MICHIGAN
Physical Map

Elevation

13000 10000 6000 3000 1800 600 0 Feet
4000   3000   1800 900   550   200 0 Meters

– – – –   State boundary

– –– – ––   International boundary

0   25   50 Miles

0   25   50   75   100 Kilometers

Lake
Michigan

Au Sable River

Houghton
Lake

River

GREAT
LAKES
PLAINS

Lake
Huron

Muskegon

L O W E R
P E N I N S U L A

Grand

River

Saint Clair River

ONTARIO

CANADA

Kalamazoo

River

Lake
Saint Clair

Detroit River

IOWA

ILLINOIS

INDIANA

OHIO

Lake
Erie

9

It's easy to find Michigan on a map of the United States by looking for a state in the shape of a mitten. The mitten is the Lower Peninsula. Its unique shape was carved out thousands of years ago by

glaciers. These large masses of ice and snow inched over both peninsulas. In some places, the glaciers were two miles thick.

The glaciers gouged huge holes in the land. As the ice and snow melted, they filled the holes with water, forming the Great Lakes—the largest system of freshwater lakes in the world. The glaciers also created thousands of smaller lakes, including Houghton, Saint Clair, and Gogebic.

Glaciers helped shape Michigan's two land regions—the Superior Upland and the Great Lakes Plains.

Colorful sandstone cliffs at Pictured Rocks National Lakeshore rise along Lake Superior.

The Superior Upland covers the western half of the Upper Peninsula. Rolling hills and a few weathered mountain ranges make the region higher and more rugged than the rest of the state.

The upland's Porcupine and Huron Mountains, both near the shores of Lake Superior, receive a lot of snow in the winter. As a result, these mountain ranges offer some of the best skiing in the Midwest. Small towns, dairy farms, and copper mines are found among the hills, pine forests, and sparkling lakes of the Superior Upland.

The Porcupine Mountains are covered by lush forests.

The Great Lakes Plains region stretches across the eastern half of the U.P. and the entire Lower Peninsula. Most of the Great Lakes Plains region is flat. The southern half of the region is the only part of the state well suited for raising crops. This area has good soil and the longest growing season in the state.

Several islands that are part of Michigan dot the waters of the Great Lakes. The Beaver Islands and the Manitou Islands are in the northern part of Lake Michigan. Bois Blanc and Round are some of the islands in Lake Huron.

At the Eastern Market in Detroit, farmers from the Great Lakes Plains region sell their produce.

One of the nation's largest herds of moose makes its home on Isle Royale.

Mackinac Island, a resort area, lies in the Straits of Mackinac. The state's largest island, Isle Royale in Lake Superior, is a national park and home to large populations of moose and wolves.

Grand River, in the Lower Peninsula, is the longest river in the state. The Au Sable, Muskegon, and Kalamazoo are other major waterways that flow through the mitten.

The U.P.'s chief rivers include the Escanaba and the Saint Marys. The Saint Marys, Saint Clair, and Detroit Rivers are important links in a shipping highway that runs from Lake Superior and Lake Michigan to the Atlantic Ocean.

Michigan's climate varies greatly from north to south. The Upper Peninsula is colder than the Lower Peninsula and receives a lot more snow. At least 160 inches of snow blanket the state's mountains every year. But in southeastern Michigan, the city of Detroit typically gets less than 30 inches of snow each year.

Winter temperatures in the northern part of the state average 15° F, while southern Michigan is usually several degrees warmer. Summers are cool in northern Michigan, with average temperatures around 65° F. In southern Michigan, summertime temperatures average 75° F.

Northern Michigan's long winters provide snowy fun for children.

White-tailed deer *(left)*; birch trees *(below)*

In the fall, a ride down Michigan's winding roads leads you past rows of colorful birch, elm, maple, aspen, and oak trees. Forests cover more than half the state. Among the trees, wild shrubs droop with raspberries, currants, gooseberries, and elderberries.

One of Michigan's nicknames, the Wolverine State, may come from the many wolverine furs sold by trappers in the area long ago. Wolverines probably never actually lived in Michigan, but the state is home to a large number of their fur-bearing cousins, including muskrat, beavers, badgers, and weasels. Deer also abound. In fact, Michigan usually has more deer than any other state except Texas.

The largest sand dune in Michigan *(above)* lies on Lake Michigan's eastern shore. According to an Ottawa and Ojibwa Indian legend, a black bear and her two cubs began swimming across the lake to escape a forest fire. The cubs grew tired and drowned, but the mother bear crawled to shore. Sad and weak from her long swim, she lay down to wait for her babies. The gods felt sorry for the mother bear and covered her with sand, creating the Sleeping Bear Dune.

From Mound Builders to Car Makers

 he state of Michigan takes its name from the Ottawa Indian word *michigama*, which means "great water." The Ottawas used the word to describe what we call Lake Michigan.

The first people to see Lake Michigan probably included the ancestors of the Ottawa Indians. About 10,000 years ago, American Indians, or Native Americans, entered the Great Lakes region from the west. Many of these early Indians settled near what later became Detroit. Others braved the harsh winds and the cold of the Upper Peninsula. People throughout what later became Michigan hunted animals and picked berries for food.

Early Michiganians ate berries like these.

The Indians in the U.P. discovered vast stores of copper just beneath the surface of the earth. These Indians were likely the first people in the Americas to mine copper and make tools from the metal.

American Indians in what later became Michigan eventually learned the skill of mound building from other Indians hundreds of miles to the south. Mound builders constructed religious and burial sites by piling earthen materials into huge heaps. Around A.D. 1500, for some unknown reason, the mound building stopped. Many of the ancient mounds still exist along the Grand River near Grand Rapids, Michigan.

By the 1600s, several groups of Indians were living throughout the Upper and Lower Peninsulas. The Ojibwa, Potawatomi, and Ottawa Indians led similar lifestyles and loosely united themselves as the

To find copper for making tools, ancient Indians dug pits deep into the ground.

Indians traveled on the Great Lakes in birchbark canoes.

Council of Three Tribes. These Native Americans handcrafted birchbark canoes. The villagers gathered wild rice, raised crops of corn and beans, and hunted deer and other animals.

Another tribe, the Menomini Indians, lived along the shores of Lake Michigan in the Upper Peninsula. Wild rice thrived in the area, and the Menomini harvested so much that they didn't need to grow crops to feed tribe members.

For generations the Indians of the two peninsulas traded food and goods with other tribes in all directions. In the early 1600s, new trading partners—the French—arrived on the scene.

For the Indians in the Great Lakes region, contact with the French started in the early 1600s. Around 1618, a young French explorer named Etienne Brulé canoed the Great Lakes, becoming the first European to set foot in the Michigan area. Soon afterward, French traders and trappers came to the area.

The Indians and French were different in many ways, but each respected the other's skills and way of life. They learned to speak each other's languages, and they participated in a trading system called the Great Huron Trade Circle.

The circle began with the Indians. They gave wolverine and beaver furs to the French. In return, the Indians got beads, pots, knives, guns, and clothing from the French. The Indians or the French used large canoes to transport the furs across a long water route to Quebec, an important trading center in what would later become Canada.

Some canoes held nearly five tons of cargo. From Quebec, the furs were sent to Europe, where they were sold at a great profit.

The Voyageur

His cart is beloved of the ploughman,
the hunter loves his gun, his hound;
The musician is a music lover—
to my canoe I'm bound.
(From the voyageur song "My Birchbark Canoe")

The canoe was everything to the voyageur. His transportation, his livelihood, his home. *Voyageurs,* the French word for "travelers," were canoeists hired by the fur companies to transport furs along the Great Huron Trade Circle. Their birchbark canoes, with a superb design copied from the Indians, were up to 40 feet long and carried several tons of crew and cargo.

The life of the voyageurs was hard. Up before sunrise, the skilled canoeists rowed all day, sometimes 15 to 18 hours straight. After years of rowing, their shoulder muscles grew thick and large.

In calm water, the voyageurs were fast. They glided along at four to six miles per hour—about one stroke per second. They could also shoot rapids, speed along creeks, and plow through the bashing waves of the Great Lakes. To get from one waterway to another or to pass a waterfall, the voyageurs portaged, or carried their canoes and cargoes overland, sometimes for dozens of miles.

The canoeists, most of whom were French Canadian, passed the hours singing French ballads about their lives and their work. These songs, a part of history, bring the voyageur back to life.

The voyageurs sang as they paddled the Great Lakes.

French fur trappers and traders worked closely with Indians.

In 1668 in the Upper Peninsula, the French established Sault Sainte Marie, the first permanent European settlement in Michigan. Later, along the Straits of Mackinac, French traders built Fort Michilimackinac. In 1701 Antoine Cadillac, a French soldier, established a fort where the city of Detroit stands today. Fort Pontchartrain du Détroit became a trading center for the entire Great Lakes region.

Several hundred people traveled from France to live in the Michigan area. Most of them were fur trappers and traders, interested mainly in business. Others were Catholic priests who came to teach the Indians about Christianity.

By this time, the British had also established fur-trading posts and **colonies,** or settlements, in other parts of North America. When France and Great Britain made war in Europe, fighting between the French and the British also occurred in North America.

French settlers established Fort Michilimackinac in 1715.

During Pontiac's war, Pontiac *(center left)* claimed he wanted to discuss an end to the fighting with British major Henry Gladwin *(center right)*. In reality Pontiac and about 300 Indians had planned a surprise attack. Gladwin had been warned of the plan ahead of time and had heavily armed his soldiers—a sight that caused the Indians to retreat.

Native Americans in the two peninsulas sided with their trading partners—the French—in what became known as the French and Indian War (1754–1763). France lost the war and gave its forts and most of its territory to the British. The British replaced the French in the fur trade. Instead of respecting the Indians, the British treated them poorly.

Fed up with British treatment, an Ottawa leader named Pontiac led the Council of Three Tribes and other Indian groups in an attack on British forts in 1763. Although the Indians won many battles, they could not overcome British forces at Detroit. Pontiac's soldiers returned to their homes, forced to accept British control of the area.

The British had hardly put down their firearms when 13 of their colonies along the Atlantic coast began preparing to fight for independence. During the American Revolution (1775–1783), the people of Detroit supplied British soldiers with food, guns, and bullets.

The British lost the revolution, and the 13 former colonies established a new country—the United States of America. The British and the Americans argued about who owned the territory that lay west and north of the United States. Some Michiganians would be calling themselves Canadian today if the British had followed a plan to claim northern Michigan for themselves. But the British kept only the area that would become Canada.

The Erie Canal

Even after boundaries were established in 1783, the British refused to leave their profitable fur-trading posts at Mackinac Island and at Detroit until 1796. Soon afterward, in 1805, the U.S. government organized the Lower Peninsula and the eastern half of the Upper Peninsula into the Territory of Michigan.

By 1820 only 7,000 Indians and 9,000 settlers were living in Michigan. Stories of swampland and poor farmland kept people in the eastern states from traveling that far west. But the construction of a canal in the state of New York changed thousands of people's minds about moving to Michigan.

The Erie Canal, completed in 1825, was a water-way built to connect Lake Erie to New York's Hudson River, which flows into the Atlantic Ocean. On the canal, people and goods from the New York area could travel easily to Michigan and back again by boat.

At first Michigan shipped only furs along the canal. But the fur trade had slowed down by the early 1830s because most of the fur-bearing animals in the territory had been killed. Wheat, flour, whiskey, and lumber eventually replaced furs.

Detroit had grown into a bustling city by the 1830s.

In the 1800s, lumberjacks competed to see who could stack the most logs on a logging sled.

By the mid-1830s, the Erie Canal had helped increase Michigan's non-Indian population from 9,000 to 175,000. The territory had more than enough residents to apply for statehood. In 1837, after agreeing to give Ohio a strip of land in southern Michigan, Michigan became the 26th state. That same year, the U.S. government gave the western half of the U.P. to Michigan. The site of the old Fort Pontchartrain du Détroit became the state capital.

Michigan had some good farmland and an abundant supply of pine trees, which meant lots of jobs for loggers. Most of the farmland and forest covered what was once the homeland of the Indians.

28

Over the years, Michigan's government had asked tribe leaders to give up most of their territory. In exchange, the U.S. government gave the Indians money and parcels of land, called **reservations,** where the Native Americans could live undisturbed by white settlers. By the mid-1800s, the last such **treaty,** or agreement, had been signed.

These Ojibwa Indians lived in a village near Sault Sainte Marie in 1850.

Locks on the Soo Canals have been in use since 1855. Ships, such as this ore carrier, still pass through them.

In 1847 Michigan's capital was moved from Detroit to Lansing, a location more central to the lumber industry. By this time, loggers were making a lot of money. Settlers were building homes on the treeless prairies west of Michigan. They needed lumber, and Michigan's pine was among the best building lumber available.

The copper and iron ore found in the western half of the U.P. also made a lot of money for the state. Copper was used to make coins, and iron ore went into cast iron and, later, steel.

But the large ships needed to carry Michigan's

metals to factories could not get past the rapids along the Saint Marys River, which connects Lakes Superior and Huron. So the state completed the Soo Canal in 1855. This deep, narrow waterway included a **lock,** or closed area, to lower and raise ships past the rapids. Later, more locks were added. The canal was divided to become the Soo Canals.

Meanwhile, the nation was undergoing many changes. In 1861 the Civil War began. Southern states formed their own country, the Confederate States of America, and fought against the Northern states, or the Union. The Union won the war in 1865.

Workers create wooden furniture from Michigan's rich supply of trees.

After the war, many types of industries grew in Michigan. By the late 1800s, Grand Rapids was famous for building furniture. Maple syrup and maple sugar, beet sugar, and cheese led the list of food products made in the state. And the U.P.'s copper mines were producing at an all-time high.

An early driver and his passenger go for a spin in a Model T Ford. The Model T was made in the Detroit area.

Progress was also being made toward the invention of the horseless carriage—better known as the automobile. The invention relied on the work of hundreds of people all over the world. But inventors in Michigan figured out not only how to make a car run but also how to assemble it cheaply enough so that people could afford to buy one.

In 1899 Ransom E. Olds opened Olds Motor Works—the first car factory in Detroit. In 1903 Henry Ford founded the Ford Motor Company, also in Detroit. Automobiles with names such as Oldsmobile and Model T were paraded down the streets of Detroit and elsewhere. Before long, Detroit was producing so many cars it became known as the Motor City.

Ford workers inspect cars at the end of a moving assembly line.

Putting the Pieces Together

In 1910 the Ford Motor Company began producing automobiles at its new plant in Highland Park, Michigan. Just three years later, workers at the plant convinced Henry Ford to experiment with a new style of production. This experiment—the moving assembly line—fueled the success of the automobile industry.

On the moving assembly line, the frame of the automobile was mounted on a slow-moving chain, and workers were stationed along the chain. As the product passed, each worker had a short amount of time to attach a specific part before the car moved on.

By using the moving assembly line, Ford produced cars faster and more cheaply. Because Ford's automobiles were less expensive, more people could afford to buy them. Making them quickly became essential. In 1910, before the moving assembly line, Ford produced about 30,000 cars. Twelve years later, that figure rose to more than 1 million.

In the early 1900s, dozens of car factories sprang up in the Michigan cities of Flint, Pontiac, and Detroit. During World War I (1914–1918), Michigan's car factories were needed to make army tanks and trucks. Wartime factory jobs attracted southerners, many of them African American, to Michigan. Factories in Michigan paid more than farms in southern states did.

During World War II (1939–1945), the U.S. military needed tanks and trucks and also airplanes.

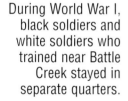

During World War I, black soldiers and white soldiers who trained near Battle Creek stayed in separate quarters.

More southerners, white and black, came to Michigan to work in the state's factories. Detroit's population alone increased by about 500,000. At least 50,000 of the newcomers were African American. By 1960 African Americans made up 9 percent of Michigan's population and 30 percent of Detroit's.

During World War II, B-24 Liberator bombers were built by Ford Motor Company's Willow Run plant.

Black people in Michigan and throughout the country had long been treated unfairly by many white people. For example, homes in some white neighborhoods were not sold to black people. And blacks were sometimes accused by police of crimes they hadn't committed. African Americans wanted to have the same rights as white people.

In July 1967, police were arresting several African Americans in Detroit when a group of angry black onlookers began to set buildings on fire and to loot stores in protest. Disturbances also erupted that week in other cities in Michigan, including Pontiac, Grand Rapids, Saginaw, and Kalamazoo.

After the riots, Michigan passed a law that made it illegal to refuse to sell a home to a person based on skin color. In addition, police and fire departments promoted black people to leadership positions, so they could help control how African Americans were being treated.

Michigan made national headlines in 1973, when President Richard Nixon named Gerald R. Ford—a native of Grand Rapids—vice president of the

United States. Less than a year later, after Nixon resigned from office, Ford became the 38th president of the United States.

Since the days of Henry Ford and Ransom Olds, the number of people who can find jobs in Michigan has depended on the success of the automobile industry. When cars are selling well, Michiganians —from factory workers to advertising executives— have jobs.

During the 1967 riots in Detroit, entire blocks of the city were burned to the ground.

1978 OLDS

1,000,000k at us now
PRIDE *and* QUALITY
DID IT AGAIN!

1,000,000th
1978 OLDSMOBILE

Many of Michigan's automobile factory workers had lost their jobs by 1980.

By 1980 competition from foreign car manufacturers had grown fierce. Michigan's factories were selling fewer cars, and thousands of Michiganians lost their jobs. The state recorded the highest number of unemployed people in the country.

To sell more cars, Detroit's automakers have been working hard to improve the quality of their products.

Since the 1990s, Michigan has also worked to attract new businesses so that the state's workers don't have to depend on the success of one industry. By 2001 the state had created 34,000 new jobs, and billions of dollars had been invested in new businesses. It also became the first state to win the Governor's Cup four times in a row, awarded for a state's successful business expansion. This gives Michiganians pride in their state and hope for continued success in the future.

The People Mover, an elevated train that transports people around Detroit's business district, has been operating since 1987.

Michiganians enjoy the peace and quiet of the outdoors at Pictured Rocks National Lakeshore.

PEOPLE & ECONOMY

Wolverines at Work and Play

hese days, Antoine Cadillac might feel out of place in the hustle and bustle of downtown Detroit. But he would feel right at home in parts of northern Michigan, where bears and deer outnumber people.

Since 1825, when the Erie Canal was built, Michigan's population has grown from about 9,000 to nearly 10 million. Much of this growth has occurred in southern Michigan, where the state's largest cities—Detroit, Grand Rapids, Warren, Flint, Sterling Heights, and Lansing (the capital)— are located. Marquette, with almost 20,000 people, is the largest city in the U.P.

Michigan also offers the excitement of city life.

Over the years, people from different parts of the world have chosen Michigan to be their new home. Many Michiganians have ancestors from Canada, France, Great Britain, Germany, Holland, Poland, Finland, Italy, Belgium, and Bulgaria. More recent **immigrants** include Canadians, Arabs, and Latinos.

More than 14 percent of Michiganians and more than 80 percent of Detroiters are African American. Native Americans make up less than 1 percent of Michigan's population. Many of them live on one of

Dancers celebrate their African heritage at the Detroit Festival of the Arts.

This Native American Michiganian dances in traditional dress at a powwow.

the state's seven reservations.

With its mix of people, Michigan has a variety of lively cultural traditions. Every weekend throughout the summer, for instance, Hart Plaza in downtown Detroit hosts a different ethnic festival featuring food, music, and dance.

During the Tulip Time Festival, the city of Holland, Michigan, honors its Dutch heritage with a parade. Participants wear Dutch outfits complete with wooden shoes. The city of Frankenmuth was built to look like a German village. People travel from miles around to taste the chicken and sausages in the town's restaurants.

Because automobiles are forbidden on Mackinac Island, some people travel in horse-drawn carriages.

Michigan is famous for its automobiles, but one place in the state doesn't even allow them! Visitors to Mackinac Island, a resort area on Lake Huron, must leave their cars behind and ride bicycles or in horse-drawn carriages. Nearby is the Mackinac Bridge, which spans the Straits of Mackinac and connects the two peninsulas. Every Labor Day, just for fun, thousands of people gather for the Mackinac Bridge Walk.

The state's museums reflect Michigan's past and look toward its future. Greenfield Village, an outdoor museum in Dearborn, was built by automobile pioneer Henry Ford. Ford arranged to move the actual homes and workplaces of some of the world's most famous inventors to the village. The Henry Ford Museum, which shares the grounds, exhibits old cars and other inventions.

Perhaps you'll invent something at the Detroit Science Center, where visitors can conduct their own experiments. Detroit is also the site of the original recording studio of Motown Records, where black musicians such as the Supremes, Michael Jackson, and Smokey Robinson started on their path to stardom.

The Michigan International Speedway near Jackson is a popular place to see car races.

Sports teams in Michigan compete with the best. Professional clubs include baseball's Detroit Tigers, basketball's Detroit Pistons, hockey's Detroit Red Wings, and football's Detroit Lions. The state's most watched college teams are the University of Michigan Wolverines and the Michigan State University Spartans. Crowds fill the bleachers when these two rivals compete.

Competition gets fierce when the Spartans meet the Wolverines on the football field.

Michigan's four seasons allow residents to participate in all types of outdoor activities. Many vacationers flock to the Upper Peninsula, far from the crowded cities. The state's lakes draw fishers, boaters, and swimmers during the spring and summer. Fall is the season for hunting and hiking. Skiing, skating, and snowmobiling are popular winter activities.

With so much to do and see, tourism is a big moneymaker for the state of Michigan. Approximately 11 million vacationers spend billions of dollars in Michigan's restaurants, campsites, and hotels and on boating, hunting, and fishing licenses each year. The waitpeople, salesclerks, and hotel desk clerks who help tourists have service jobs. Many of the service jobs in the Detroit area revolve around the automobile industry. For example, some salespeople buy and sell cars and car parts. Altogether, service jobs in Michigan employ 62 percent of the state's workers.

A swimmer enjoys the rushing waters of the Little Carp River in the Upper Peninsula.

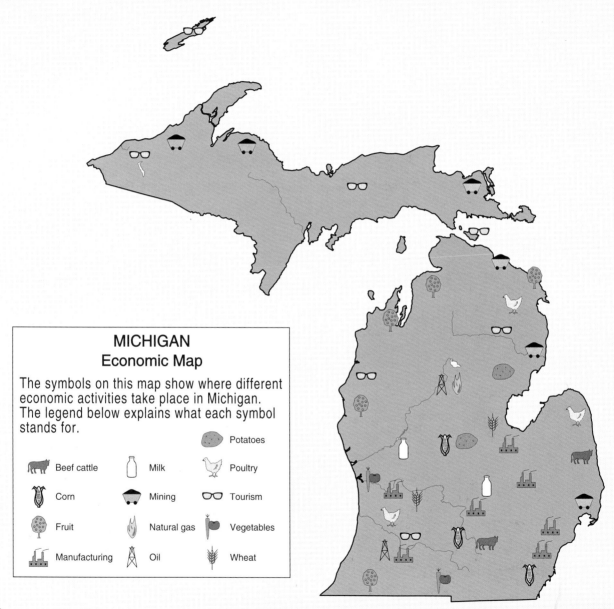

MICHIGAN
Economic Map

The symbols on this map show where different economic activities take place in Michigan. The legend below explains what each symbol stands for.

Beef cattle	Milk	Potatoes			
Corn	Mining	Poultry			
Fruit	Natural gas	Tourism			
Manufacturing	Oil	Vegetables			
		Wheat			

One of the top manufacturing states, Michigan employs about 19 percent of its workforce with manufacturing jobs. General Motors Corporation, Ford Motor Company, and DaimlerChrysler Corporation are all headquartered in or near Detroit.

Computers, tools, and car parts are also made in the state. Food products rank next in importance. Battle Creek has kept its title as the Cereal Bowl of the World by making more breakfast cereals than any other city worldwide. Workers throughout the state also process fruits, vegetables, and baby food.

Cars are fitted with doors near the end of an assembly line.

Michigan farmers raise animals such as calves *(above left)* as well as fruits and vegetables *(above right).*

Compared to manufacturing, the number of workers employed in agriculture is small—only 2 percent. Farmers in the state grow corn, soybeans, wheat, potatoes, berries, apples, and other fruits. Michigan's farmers also raise livestock, including dairy cattle, beef cattle, hogs, turkeys, and chickens.

Miners in the U.P. supply one-fourth of the iron ore needed to make the nation's steel. Large deposits of copper also exist, but removing the copper usually costs more than the metal is worth. Several natural gas fields and oil wells dot the northern half of the Lower Peninsula.

On the Great Lakes, the scene has changed since the 1600s. Freighters have replaced canoes, mariners have replaced voyageurs, and iron ore and wheat have replaced furs. Many of Michigan's products are shipped to Canada, the East Coast, and to northern Europe. Ships leave port cities along their route and stop at Detroit, one of the busiest ports in the country.

Detroit's founder, Antoine Cadillac, wouldn't recognize the freighter-filled Detroit River. He probably wouldn't even be able to locate the original site of his Fort Pontchartrain du Détroit. But if the Frenchman were around today, he might enjoy a ride in the back of a horseless carriage . . . a Cadillac maybe?

A ship on the Detroit River passes downtown Detroit.

Michiganians appreciate the natural beauty of their state's lakes and rivers.

THE ENVIRONMENT

Polluted Water, Toxic Fish

Every fishing license sold in Michigan comes with a booklet warning anglers that some fish caught in the state may not be safe to eat. Many of the state's fish are contaminated with **hazardous wastes**—metals and chemicals that in large doses can harm or even kill living things. Common hazardous wastes in Michigan's lakes and rivers include mercury and polychlorinated biphenyls (PCBs).

Mercury, a poisonous liquid metal, occurs naturally in soil and rocks. The metal is mined for use in products such as thermometers, fluorescent light bulbs, batteries, and certain medicines and fertilizers. At one time, mercury was added to paints.

At some lakes and rivers in Michigan, signs are posted warning people that the water is too polluted to swim in.

If mercury and PCBs are mixed in with other garbage, they cannot be found and destroyed.

PCBs, a family of poisonous chemicals, were once used in paints, plastics, and electrical devices. After the dangers of PCBs became known in the 1970s, they were banned. But their harmful effects still linger.

Mercury and PCBs get into Michigan's lakes and rivers in several ways. Old paints and other goods containing PCBs and mercury are still being used. The hazardous wastes found in old and new products gradually evaporate into the air. Rain carries the wastes down into waterways. Mercury also seeps from rocks and soil directly into lakes and rivers.

Much of the mercury and PCBs in household products can be destroyed if properly burned in hazardous waste incinerators, or large furnaces. But many people throw old batteries, paint, and other contaminated products into their household garbage. For this reason, a lot of mercury and PCBs never make it to hazardous waste incinerators.

Coal is burned by the ton at power plants like this one in River Rouge, Michigan, in order to create electricity for homes and other buildings.

When Michigan burns garbage in regular incinerators, products containing mercury or PCBs give off large amounts of toxic, or poisonous, gases. Power plants that burn coal, which contains small amounts of mercury, also produce toxic gas. The poisonous gases float in the air until rainwater carries them down into lakes and rivers.

In the past, industries dumped unneeded mercury- and PCB-contaminated materials directly into rivers and lakes. The wastes piled up in the sediment on the bottom of the waterways. Laws prevent industries from discharging PCBs, but small amounts of mercury can still be dumped.

Fishers have to be careful to avoid eating contaminated fish, which may cause health problems.

Once PCBs and mercury are in the water, small insects that live at the bottom of the lakes and rivers absorb some of the hazardous waste. Small fish eat the contaminated insects and also become contaminated. The cycle continues when large fish eat the small fish.

When people eat contaminated fish, they also take in the toxic materials. Over time, the mercury and PCBs build up in the human body, which is unable to digest and get rid of these poisons.

Scientists are studying the harmful effects of mercury and PCBs on people's health. They have found that by eating contaminated fish, pregnant women risk harming their unborn children, who may eventually suffer health problems or learning disorders. Women who eat contaminated fish long before becoming pregnant may still pass on mercury and PCBs to their children.

In most ways, eating fish is good for your health. Fish is low in calories and fat—too much of which can lead to heart disease. Fish is also high in protein. To get these benefits without the dangers of mercury and PCBs, people can take precautions.

Limiting the amount of fish eaten to less than 12 ounces per week can help. After catching or buying fish, trim off the fat, where PCBs tend to collect. Baking, broiling, or grilling your catch on a rack allows even more fat to drip off as the fish cooks.

People in Michigan are experimenting with different ways to reduce the levels of PCBs and mercury in Michigan's waterways. New, specially designed incinerators can destroy 99 percent of the PCBs in hazardous waste products. And fitting these incinerators with filters could keep mercury from escaping. These solutions, however, are expensive.

Another idea is to feed nutrients to a PCB-destroying bacteria that is already present in Michigan's waterways, increasing its numbers and the amount of PCBs it can destroy. But no one knows for sure what effects this method would have on the water.

Another way to clean bodies of water may be to dredge, or dig up, riverbeds and lakebeds to collect the PCB-contaminated soil. This process would stir up old PCBs, causing them to rise up into the water. Without dredging, new sediment containing fewer PCBs would settle on top of the old sediment and keep living things from absorbing as much of the poison.

Fishing remains a popular sport in Michigan for all ages.

All Michiganians can help by separating products that contain PCBs or mercury from the rest of their trash. Michigan may pass laws that require people to pay a deposit when buying batteries and other products that contain mercury. When the consumer returns the product, the deposit is returned and the mercury is sent to a hazardous waste incinerator or a recycling center.

By properly disposing of hazardous wastes, Michiganians have already lowered the amount of mercury and

PCBs in certain fish by at least six times since the 1970s. The levels of contamination are still high, but Michiganians are working to further reduce them. In the meantime, those who limit how much fish they eat and who prepare the fish properly can keep fishing from becoming a dangerous sport.

Michiganians are working to ensure that future generations have access to clean and safe water.

ALL ABOUT MICHIGAN

Young Michiganians play at one of their state's beaches.

Fun Facts

Sometimes called the Water Wonderland, Michigan has more miles of shoreline (3,288 miles) than the Atlantic coast of the United States.

Michigan makes more passenger cars and trucks than any other state in the United States.

Before 1848 people who lived in Michigan were called Michiganians. In 1848 Abraham Lincoln (who later became a U.S. president) jokingly called the state's residents Michiganders. People in modern Michigan use both terms, and they still argue about which is correct.

By inventing and selling cold breakfast cereals, W.K. Kellogg and C.W. Post turned the small town of Battle Creek, Michigan, into the Cereal Bowl of the World in the early 1900s.

Michigan was once governed by a politician so young he was called the Boy Governor. Stevens T. Mason took over the governorship of the Territory of Michigan in 1831, when he was only 19 years old.

Colon, Michigan, was named for the colon, a punctuation mark. The town's founders decided to name the town after the first word they saw when they opened a dictionary. "Colon" was that word.

Detroit has a floating post office. The *Joseph J. Hogan,* a 41-foot boat, delivers mail to moving ships in Detroit's harbor.

Cereal from Battle Creek, Michigan, feeds the world.

STATE SONG

Michigan does not have an official state song. But the song "Michigan, My Michigan" is often used to celebrate the state. The song borrows the melody of the German Christmas carol "O Tannenbaum," as do state songs from Maryland, New Jersey, and Iowa.

MICHIGAN, MY MICHIGAN

Words by Douglas Malloch

A song to thee, fair State of mine, Mich - i - gan, my Mich - i - gan; but

great - er song than this is thine, Mich - i - gan, my Mich - i - gan; The

whis - per of the for - est tree, The thun - der of the in - land sea, U -

nite in one grand sym - pho - ny of Mich - i - gan my Mich - i - gan.

You can hear "Michigan, My Michigan" by visiting this website:
<http://www.50states.com/songs/michigan.htm>

A MICHIGAN RECIPE

Did you know that Michigan leads the nation in blueberry production? Nearly 45 percent of the blueberries eaten in the United States are grown in the Great Lakes State. On a hot summer day in Michigan—or anywhere—cool blueberry sherbert hits the spot!

MICHIGAN CREAMY BLUEBERRY SHERBERT

3 cups fresh blueberries
3 cups milk
¾ cup sugar (add more or less to taste)
2 tablespoons lemon juice

1. Pour milk into ice cube trays. Place blueberries on flat tray. Place milk and berries in freezer until frozen.
2. Remove milk and fruit from freezer. Blend together in food processor or blender by alternately adding milk cubes and fruit.
3. When mixture is slushy, add sugar and lemon juice. Continue blending until mixed but still slushy and frozen.
4. Serve immediately if firm enough. If too soft, refreeze sherbert, and let it soften at room temperature before serving.

Makes eight servings.

HISTORICAL TIMELINE

8,000 B.C. Indians enter the area that later became Michigan.

A.D. 1618 Etienne Brulé becomes the first European to visit the Michigan area.

1668 Sault Sainte Marie, a French settlement, is established.

1701 Antoine Cadillac founds Detroit.

1754 The French and Indian War (1754–1763) begins.

1763 Pontiac's War takes place.

1796 The last of the British fur traders leave the Michigan area.

1805 The U.S. government establishes the Territory of Michigan.

1825 The Erie Canal is completed.

1837 Michigan becomes the 26th state.

1847 Michigan's capital changes from Detroit to Lansing.

1855 The Soo Canal is completed.

1861 The Civil War (1861–1865) begins, and Michigan sides with the North.

1899 Ransom E. Olds founds Olds Motor Works.

1901 John F. and Horace Elgin Dodge establish their automotive company, Dodge Brothers.

1903 Henry Ford opens the Ford Motor Company.

1914 World War I (1914–1918) begins, increasing the number of factory jobs in Michigan and attracting African Americans from the south.

1939 World War II (1939–1945) begins. More factory jobs are created in Michigan.

1967 Racial tension leads to riots in Detroit and other major Michigan cities.

1974 Michiganian Gerald Ford becomes the 38th U.S. president.

1987 The People Mover begins operating in Detroit.

2001 Michigan becomes the first state to win the Governor's Cup four years in a row for successful business expansion.

OUTSTANDING MICHIGANIANS

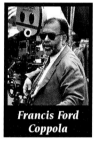

Madonna

Madonna Louise Veronica Ciccone (born 1958), from Bay City, Michigan, best known only by her first name, is a singer, dancer, and actress. Madonna's hit albums include *The Immaculate Collection, Ray of Light*, and *Music*. The superstar has played leading roles in several films, including *Evita* and *The Next Best Thing*.

Francis Ford Coppola

Francis Ford Coppola (born 1939) is a director, writer, and producer from Detroit. In 1974 Coppola won an Academy Award for directing *The Godfather, Part II*. Coppola's other films include *Apocalypse Now* and *The Rainmaker*.

John F. (1864–1920) and **Horace Elgin** (1868–1920) **Dodge** were brothers who made their fortune by producing automotive parts and Dodge cars. John was a shrewd businessman while Horace organized the technical and mechanical aspects of their successful Detroit company, Dodge Brothers. The Dodges were born in Niles, Michigan.

Gerald R. Ford

Gerald R. Ford (born 1913) was the first person to become president of the United States without being elected to either the vice presidency or the presidency. President Richard Nixon appointed Ford to be vice president after Spiro Agnew resigned in 1973. When Nixon resigned in 1974, Ford became the 38th president. Ford grew up in Grand Rapids, Michigan.

Henry Ford

Henry Ford (1863–1947), born in Dearborn, forever changed the American way of life with the development of the affordable Model T, also known as the Tin Lizzie. Ford founded the Ford Motor Company in 1903.

Daniel Gerber (1898–1974), of Fremont, Michigan, was a business-man who began mass-producing baby food in 1928 after seeing how long it took his wife to strain peas for their seven-month-old daughter. Less than 20 years later, the Gerber Products Company was selling 5 million jars of baby food a day.

Daniel Gerber

Berry Gordy Jr. (born 1929), founded the Motown Record Corporation in 1959. Motown, which became the largest independently owned record company in the world, launched numerous black musicians into successful careers. Gordy, from Detroit, was inducted into the Rock and Roll Hall of Fame in 1988.

Berry Gordy

Judith Guest (born 1936), a native of Detroit, is an author who wrote the best-selling book *Ordinary People*, which was made into an Oscar-winning movie. Guest also wrote *Second Heaven* and *Errands*.

Gordie Howe (born 1928) holds the National Hockey League record for most seasons played (26) and most games played (1,767). Howe began his professional career at the age of 18 and played right wing for the Detroit Red Wings until 1971.

Gordie Howe

Lee Iacocca (born 1924) became president of the Ford Motor Company after producing stylish, affordable cars such as the Mustang. In 1978, after 32 years with Ford, Iacocca became president of the Chrysler Corporation, where he helped the failing automobile company survive. He retired in 1992.

Earvin "Magic" Johnson Jr. (born 1959), from Lansing, is a former basketball superstar. He was drafted by the Los Angeles Lakers in 1979 while he was a student at Michigan State University. Johnson became one of basketball's greatest guards. He retired in 1991, after he tested positive for the virus that causes AIDS.

Magic Johnson

Malcolm X

Malcolm X (Malcolm Little) (1925–1965), a prominent member of the Black Muslims (a black nationalist group), stressed the beauty and value of being black. Malcolm X, who grew up in Lansing, was shot and killed after later disagreeing with and speaking out against the Black Muslims.

Terry McMillan (born 1951), from Port Huron, is a popular African American author whose novels focus on the lives of black women in the United States. Her most successful books include *Waiting to Exhale* and *How Stella Got Her Groove Back*, both of which were made into movies.

Harriet Quimby

Harriet Quimby (1875–1912) was the first woman in the United States to earn a pilot's license. She went on to become the first woman to fly over the English Channel. Quimby died in a tragic flying accident. She is believed to have grown up either in Coldwater or Arcadia, Michigan.

Gilda Radner

Gilda Radner (1946–1989), from Detroit, was a gifted comedienne. As one of the original cast members of the late-night comedy show *Saturday Night Live*, she often played wacky characters such as Roseanne Roseannadanna and Baba Wawa. Radner also played comedic roles in several movies, including *Haunted Honeymoon*.

Walter P. Reuther

Walter P. Reuther (1907–1970) moved to Detroit in 1926 and helped organize the United Auto Workers (UAW), the automobile industry's first workers' union. As the UAW's president from 1946 to 1970, Reuther helped autoworkers gain pay increases and unemployment benefits.

Diana Ross (born 1944), a singer from Detroit, soared to fame with the Supremes, a leading pop group of the 1960s. The group produced many popular songs like "Stop in the Name of Love" and "Back in My Arms." After leaving the Supremes in 1970, Ross continued to record hit songs, including "Endless Love."

Diana Ross

Bob Seger (born 1945) is a rock singer and songwriter from Ann Arbor, Michigan. Bob Seger and the Silver Bullet Band made many successful albums. Their hit songs include "Shame on the Moon."

Tom Selleck (born 1945) starred in the television series *Magnum, P.I.* from 1980 to 1988 and later appeared on the television series *Friends.* Selleck has had roles in several films, including *Three Men and a Baby* and *In and Out.* Selleck is originally from Detroit.

Lily Tomlin

Lily Tomlin (born 1939), a comedienne from Detroit, played a telephone switchboard operator and a five-year-old girl on the comedy show *Rowan & Martin's Laugh-In* in the early 1970s. Tomlin has also starred in several films, including *Tea with Mussolini.*

Chris Van Allsburg (born 1949), a children's book writer and illustrator from Grand Rapids, has won Caldecott Awards for his illustrations in *Jumanji* and *The Polar Express.*

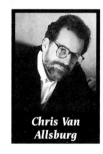
Chris Van Allsburg

Stevie Wonder (born 1950), a Grammy Award–winning musician, was born in Saginaw, Michigan, and grew up in Detroit. Blind since infancy, Wonder recorded his first song at age 13. His hits include "Ebony and Ivory" and "I Just Called to Say I Love You."

Coleman Young (1918–1997), mayor of Detroit from 1974 to 1994, served Detroiters longer than any other mayor in the city's history. Young became one of the first blacks to be elected mayor in a city with a population exceeding 1 million.

Coleman Young

FACTS-AT-A-GLANCE

Nickname: Wolverine State

Song: "Michigan, My Michigan"

Motto: *Si quaeris peninsulam amoenam, circumspice* (If You Seek a Pleasant Peninsula, Look about You)

Flower: apple blossom

Tree: white pine

Bird: robin

Fish: brook trout

Reptile: painted turtle

Stone: Petoskey stone

Gem: chlorastrolite

Date and ranking of statehood: January 26, 1837, the 26th state

Capital: Lansing

Area: 56,809 square miles

Rank in area, nationwide: 22nd

Average January temperature: 20° F

Average July temperature: 69° F

In the center of Michigan's flag, a blue shield shows the state's grassy plains and lakes. Natural beauty is also part of the state's motto *(bottom center),* which praises Michigan's beauty.

POPULATION GROWTH

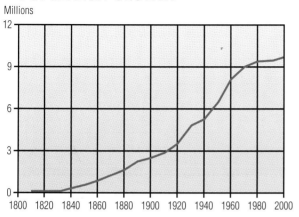

This chart shows how Michigan's population has grown from 1810 to 2000.

On the state seal, an elk and moose symbolizing Michigan support a shield with the Latin word *Tuebor,* meaning *I will defend.* The bald eagle represents the authority of the United States over state governments.

Population: 9,938,444 (2000 census)

Rank in population, nationwide: 8th

Major cities and populations: (2000 census) Detroit (951,270), Grand Rapids (197,800), Warren (138,247), Flint (124,943), Sterling Heights (124,471)

U.S. senators: 2

U.S. representatives: 15

Electoral votes: 17

Natural resources: copper, gypsum, iron ore, limestone, natural gas, petroleum, salt, sand and gravel, shale, soil

Agricultural products: apples, beef, blueberries, carrots, cherries, corn, dry beans, hogs, milk, onions, potatoes, soybeans, sugar beets, turkeys, wheat

Fishing industry: catfish, chubs, lake herring, lake trout, salmon, whitefish, yellow perch

Manufactured goods: airplane engines, baby food, boats, breakfast cereal, buses, cars, computers, furniture, hardware, machine parts, medicines, tanks, trucks

WHERE MICHIGANIANS WORK

Services—62 percent (services includes jobs in trade; community, social, and personal services; finance, insurance, and real estate; transportation, communication, and utilities)

Manufacturing—19 percent

Government—12 percent

Construction—5 percent

Agriculture—2 percent

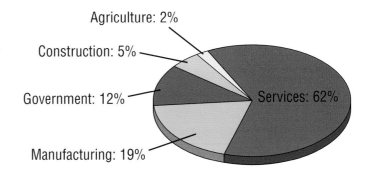

Agriculture: 2%
Construction: 5%
Government: 12%
Manufacturing: 19%
Services: 62%

GROSS STATE PRODUCT

Services—58 percent

Manufacturing—26 percent

Government—11 percent

Construction—4 percent

Agriculture—1 percent

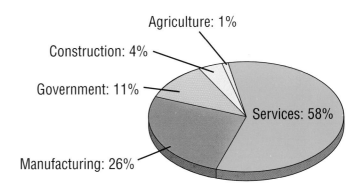

Agriculture: 1%
Construction: 4%
Government: 11%
Manufacturing: 26%
Services: 58%

MICHIGAN WILDLIFE

Mammals: badger, black bear, deer, mink, muskrat, opossum, rabbit, raccoon, red fox, skunk, squirrel, weasel

Birds: duck, egret, falcon, goose, grouse, hawk, heron, owl, pheasant, sparrow, warbler, woodpecker

Reptiles and amphibians: American toad, bullfrog, garter snake, painted turtle, salamander, snapping turtle, treefrog

Fish: bass, catfish, crappie, perch, pike, salmon, trout, walleye

Trees: aspen, beech, birch, cedar, fir, hemlock, maple, oak, pine, spruce

Wild plants: bittersweet, clematis, cranberry, fern, gooseberry, grape, lady's slipper, moss, raspberry, rose

A hiker explores Isle Royale National Park.

PLACES TO VISIT

Detroit Institute of Arts, Detroit
   With more than 60,000 works of art, this museum is the sixth largest of its kind in the United States. The museum's collection includes works from around the world, from ancient times to the 1900s.

Greenfield Village, Dearborn
   Restored by Henry Ford, this group of historic buildings and landmarks gives visitors a taste of Michigan's past. Ford brought buildings like Thomas Edison's workshop and Noah Webster's house to the village so visitors could see how these famous people lived. Next to the village is the Henry Ford Museum, which includes many early Ford cars.

Kellogg's Cereal City USA, Battle Creek
   This museum and entertainment center features a reproduction of a cereal assembly line, interactive exhibits about cereal making, and performances by some of the characters that have appeared on Kellogg's cereal boxes.

Mackinac Island
   Located between Michigan's Upper and Lower Peninsulas, this resort island is a favorite spot for nature and history lovers alike. The island is home to Michigan's first state park, the historic Fort Mackinac, and several living-history museums.

Michigan Historical Center, Lansing

This is the place to go to learn about Michigan's history, from prehistoric times to the present. Visitors to the Historical Center's museum can tour a 1930s bungalow, see a pink refrigerator and stove from the 1950s, and look at some of the first cars made in America, called horseless carriages.

Pictured Rocks National Lakeshore, near Munising

Located along Lake Superior's shoreline, this national park features cliffs, beaches, sand dunes, waterfalls, and a forest. There are also lakes, ponds, and streams for fishing and boating.

Sanilac Petroglyphs State Historic Site, Bad Axe

Native American artists made carvings called petroglyphs in sandstone rocks near the Cass River. These carvings show much about the Indians who once lived in Michigan.

Seney National Wildlife Refuge, Seney

Hundreds of different birds, fish, mammals, and plants are protected in this large wildlife preserve. The refuge includes visitor trails for walking, biking, and driving.

Sleeping Bear Dunes National Lakeshore, near Empire

Enormous sand dunes rise at the shore of Lake Michigan in this state park. Visitors can also stroll along the beach or through forests of birch, pine, beech, and maple.

Soo Canals at Sault Sainte Marie

Since the canal opened in 1855, these historic canals have allowed ships to travel between Lake Huron and Lake Superior. The canal at Sault Sainte Marie is named Saint Marys Falls Canal and Locks, and it runs almost 1.4 miles.

ANNUAL EVENTS

Erie Ice Daze, Brownstown—*January*

U.P. 200 Sled Dog Championship, Marquette—*February*

Maple Syrup Festival, Shepherd—*April*

Tulip Time Festival, Holland—*May*

Detroit Grand Prix—*June*

National Cherry Festival, Traverse City—*July*

Colonial Life Weekend, Flint—*August*

Ford Detroit International Jazz Festival—*August–September*

Red Flannel Festival, Cedar Springs—*September–October*

Annual Holiday Light Parade, Milan—*December*

LEARN MORE ABOUT MICHIGAN

BOOKS

General

Fradin, Dennis Brindell. *Michigan.* Chicago: Children's Press, 1996.

Hintz, Martin. *Michigan.* New York: Children's Press, 1998. For older readers.

Special Interest

Aretha, David. *The Michigan Wolverines Football Team.* Berkeley Heights, NJ: Enslow Publishers Inc., 1999. Covers the history of the University of Michigan's football team, including its major victories and its best-known players and coaches.

Gould, William. *VGM's Business Portraits: Kellogg's.* Lincolnwood, IL: VGM Career Horizons, 1997. Using the Kellogg Company as an example, Gould explains what makes a business successful.

Greenberg, Keith Elliot. *Magic Johnson: Champion with a Cause.* Minneapolis, MN: Lerner Publications Company, 1992. This biography follows the life of Michigan native Magic Johnson, a former basketball superstar and a leader in raising awareness of HIV, the virus that causes AIDS.

Mitchell, Barbara. *We'll Race You Henry: A Story about Henry Ford.* Minneapolis, MN: Carolrhoda Books, Inc., 1988. Learn about the inventor of the Model T and the birth of the automotive age.

Fiction

Martin, Terri. *A Family Trait*. New York: Holiday House, 1999. For her Easter vacation, 11-year-old Iris visits her grandparents on their farm in Michigan. Soon she and her friends are caught up in a local murder mystery, but Iris learns more than she bargains for.

Pfitsch, Patricia Curtis. *Keeper of the Light*. New York: Simon & Schuster, 1997. After Faith's father dies in a drowning accident, Faith and her family must move away from their home on Lake Superior in Michigan. Faith quickly learns she is not meant for town life or girlish ways.

Whelan, Gloria. *Forgive the River, Forgive the Sky*. Grand Rapids, MI: W. B. Eerdmans, 1998. In northern Michigan, 12-year-old Lily struggles to accept the loss of her father after he dies in their favorite river. While she recovers, Lily befriends a paraplegic former pilot and helps him come to terms with his own loss.

Whelan, Gloria. *Next Spring An Oriole*. New York: Random House, 1987. In 1837, 10-year-old Libby Mitchell and her family pack up their covered wagon and set off on a trail from Virginia to the Michigan frontier. Along the way they meet other settlers and are introduced to the Potawatomi Indians who live on the land.

WEBSITES

Michigan
<http://www.michigan.gov/>
Michigan's official website includes information about the state's government, economy, technology, and education.

Travel Michigan
<http://travel.michigan.org>
Michigan's official tourism site helps travelers plan their trips in Michigan. It offers information about events, destinations, and activities for all four seasons.

Detroit Free Press
<http://www.freep.com/>
Keep up with current events in Detroit by reading the online version of one of its daily newspapers, the *Detroit Free Press.*

Kids Discover Michigan
<http://www.sos.state.mi.us/kidspage/index.html>
This site, run by the Michigan secretary of state's office, teaches kids about the state's government, history, symbols, and more. Viewers can also play Michigan-related games.

PRONUNCIATION GUIDE

Brulé, Etienne (broo-LAY, ay-TYEHN)

Gogebic (goh-GEE-bihk)

Houghton (HOH-tuhn)

Isle Royale (eyel ROY-uhl)

Kalamazoo (kal-uh-muh-ZOO)

Mackinac (MAK-uh-naw)

Michilimackinac (MIHSH-uh-lee-MAK-uh-naw)

Ottawa (AHT-uh-wuh)

Pontchartrain du Détroit (PAHN-chuhr-trayn doo dee-TROYT)

Potawatomi (paht-uh-WAHT-uh-mee)

Sault Sainte Marie (soo saynt muh-REE)

A skier glides across Belle Isle, near downtown Detroit.

GLOSSARY

colony: a territory ruled by a country some distance away

glacier: a large body of ice and snow that moves slowly over land

Great Lakes: a chain of five lakes in Canada and the northern United States. They are Lakes Superior, Michigan, Huron, Erie, and Ontario.

hazardous waste: chemicals and other wastes that can harm living things or the environment. Hazardous wastes include materials that can poison, explode, burn flesh, start a fire, or carry disease.

immigrant: a person who moves into a foreign country and settles there

lock: an enclosed, water-filled chamber in a canal or river used to raise or lower boats beyond the site of a waterfall. Boats can enter the lock through gates at either end.

peninsula: a stretch of land almost completely surrounded by water

reservation: public land set aside by the government to be used by Native Americans

treaty: an agreement between two or more groups, usually having to do with peace or trade

INDEX

PHOTO ACKNOWLEDGMENTS

Cover photographs by © W. Cody/CORBIS (left) and © Kevin Fleming/CORBIS (right). PresentationMaps.com, pp. 1, 8, 9, 48; © L. Clarke/CORBIS, pp. 2–3; © James L. Amos/CORBIS, p. 3; © Eye Ubiquitous/CORBIS, pp. 4 (detail), 7 (detail), 17 (detail), 41 (detail), 53 (detail); © Stephen Graham Photography, p. 6; © Ilene MacDonald/Root Resources, p. 7; John Gerlach/Dembinsky Photo, p. 10; © John & Ann Mahan, pp. 11, 13, 14, 17, 47, 56, 59; © Dennis Cox, pp. 12, 42, 43; © Jerry Hennen, pp. 15 (left), 44; Olive Glasgow, p. 15 (right); Ken Scott/Dembinsky Photo, p. 16; Library of Congress, pp. 18, 35, 66 (bottom), 68 (second from top); Muskegon County Museum, pp. 19; National Archives Canada, Ottawa (C-2774), p. 21; Courtesy State Archives of Michigan, pp. 22, 28, 29, 34, 37, 38; Bentley Historical Library, University of Michigan, p. 23; Burton Historical Collection of the Detroit Public Library, p. 24; Independent Picture Service, pp. 26, 68 (bottom); © The Detroit Institute of Arts, Gift of the Fred Sanders Company in memory of its founder, Fred Sanders, p. 27; © James P. Rowan, p. 30; Grand Rapids Public Library—Michigan Room, p. 31; © Hulton-Deutsch Collection/CORBIS, p. 32; Ford Motor Company, pp. 33, 49; © W. Cody/CORBIS, p. 39; © Jim West, pp. 40, 51, 55, 73, 80; Roger Bickel/New England Stock Photo, p. 41; Sharon Cummings/Dembinsky Photo, p. 45; © ALLSPORT USA/Darron R. Silva, p. 46; © Monica V. Brown, p. 50 (left); Greg Ryan/Sally Beyer, p. 50 (right); © Conrad Zobel/CORBIS, p. 52; David Kenyon, Michigan Department of Natural Resources, p. 53; © Jerry Boucher, p. 54; Diane Cooper, p. 58; Michigan Travel Bureau, p. 60; George Karn, p. 61; Tim Seeley, pp. 63, 71, 72; © Reuters NewMedia Inc./CORBIS, p. 66 (top); Hollywood Book & Poster Co., pp. 66 (second from top), 68 (second from bottom), 69 (top, second from top); The White House, p. 66 (second from bottom); Gerber Products, p. 67 (top); Gordy Company, p. 67 (second from top); Brantford Expositor, p. 67 (second from bottom); Los Angeles Lakers, p. 67 (bottom); Schomburg Center for Research in Black Culture, p. 68 (top); Jan Bindas, p. 69 (second from bottom); Public Information, City of Detroit, p. 69 (bottom); Jean Matheny, p. 70 (top).